The ★ ★
UNITED
STATES
PRESIDENTS

★ ★ Rutherford B. ★ ★

HAYES

BreAnn Rumsch

Big Buddy Books

An Imprint of Abdo Publishing
abdopublishing.com

abdopublishing.com

Published by Abdo Publishing, a division of ABDO, PO Box 398166, Minneapolis, Minnesota 55439.
Copyright © 2017 by Abdo Consulting Group, Inc. International copyrights reserved in all countries. No part of this book may be reproduced in any form without written permission from the publisher. Big Buddy Books™ is a trademark and logo of Abdo Publishing.

Printed in the United States of America, North Mankato, Minnesota
062016
092016

Design: Sarah DeYoung, Mighty Media, Inc.
Production: Mighty Media, Inc.
Editor: Liz Salzmann
Cover Photograph: Corbis
Interior Photographs: Alamy (pp. 7, 15, 19); Getty Images (p. 13); Library of Congress (pp. 5, 7, 17, 23, 25); North Wind (p. 21); Public Domain (pp. 27, 29); Rutherford B. Hayes Presidential Center (pp. 6, 9, 11)

Cataloging-in-Publication Data

Names: Rumsch, BreAnn, author.
Title: Rutherford B. Hayes / by BreAnn Rumsch.
Description: Minneapolis, MN : Abdo Publishing, [2017] | Series: United States presidents | Includes bibliographical references and index.
Identifiers: LCCN 2015957544 | ISBN 9781680780994 (lib. bdg.) | ISBN 9781680775198 (ebook)
Subjects: LCSH: Hayes, Rutherford B. (Rutherford Birchard), 1822-1893--Juvenile literature. | Presidents--United States--Biography--Juvenile literature. | United States--Politics and government--1877-1881--Juvenile literature.
Classification: DDC 973.8/3092 [B]--dc23
LC record available at http://lccn.loc.gov/2015957544

Contents

Rutherford B. Hayes

Rutherford B. Hayes was the nineteenth president of the United States. During the **American Civil War**, Hayes joined the **Union** army. He fought bravely in many battles.

After the war, Hayes entered **politics**. He served in the US House of **Representatives**. Later, he became governor of Ohio.

During his presidency, Hayes ended **Reconstruction**. He also worked to improve the **civil service**. Hayes was an honest leader who loved his country.

Timeline

1822
On October 4,
Rutherford Birchard Hayes
was born in Delaware, Ohio.

1852
On December 30,
Hayes married
Lucy Ware Webb.

1842
Hayes finished
Kenyon College
in Gambier, Ohio.

1861
On April 12, the
American Civil War
began. Hayes joined
the **Union** army.

1867

Hayes was elected governor of Ohio.

1877

In March, Hayes became the nineteenth US president.

1865

In December, Hayes joined the US House of **Representatives**.

1893

Rutherford B. Hayes died on January 17.

7

Early Years

Rutherford Birchard Hayes was born on October 4, 1822, in Delaware, Ohio. He was called Rud. Growing up, Rud attended schools in Ohio and Connecticut.

Rud was a good student. He went to Kenyon College in Gambier, Ohio. He finished in 1842.

★ FAST FACTS ★

Born: October 4, 1822

Wife: Lucy Ware Webb (1831–1889)

Children: eight

Political Party: Republican

Age at Inauguration: 54

Years Served: 1877–1881

Vice President: William A. Wheeler

Died: January 17, 1893, age 70

Rud (*left*)
with two of his
classmates at
Kenyon College

9

Law and Politics

Hayes went on to attend Harvard Law School in Cambridge, Massachusetts. He finished in 1845. Hayes moved to Cincinnati, Ohio in 1849. There, he opened a law office.

Meanwhile, Hayes had met Lucy Ware Webb. They were married on December 30, 1852. The Hayeses had eight children.

In 1856, Hayes helped establish Ohio's first **Republican** Party branch. In 1858, he was elected city **solicitor**. As solicitor, he represented the city in court cases.

Rutherford and Lucy Hayes
on their wedding day

Civil War Soldier

On April 12, 1861, the **American Civil War** began. Hayes joined the **Union** army. On September 14, 1862, Hayes was wounded at the Battle of South Mountain. But he soon returned to the war.

Hayes continued to fight for the Union. He was wounded four more times. Then in December 1864, he was made a general. On April 9, 1865, the Civil War ended. Soon after, Hayes left the army.

Hayes liked being in the army. He was proud to fight for the freedom of all people.

Congressman

In December 1865, Hayes joined the US House of **Representatives**. In Congress, Hayes worked to secure the rights of freed slaves.

In June 1866, Hayes voted for the Fourteenth **Amendment**. This amendment made all former slaves US citizens.

In 1867, he voted for the **Reconstruction** Acts. These acts required Southern states to write new **constitutions**. They had to give voting rights to African-American men. The states also had to accept the Fourteenth Amendment.

Hayes was reelected to Congress in 1866.

15

Secretary of War Edwin M. Stanton was in charge of the **Reconstruction** Acts. President Andrew Johnson did not agree with the acts. So, many congressmen worried Johnson would fire Stanton.

This led Hayes and other congressmen to pass a new act. The act said the president needed the Senate's agreement to fire government officers. President Johnson tried to fire Stanton anyway.

So, in 1868, Congress voted to **impeach** President Johnson. However, Hayes was not there to vote. He had returned to Ohio to campaign for governor.

Andrew Johnson was president from 1865 to 1869.

Ohio Governor

Hayes became governor of Ohio in 1867. Governor Hayes worked to make the **civil service** better. He also wanted Ohio to have a state **university**.

In 1869, Hayes was reelected. During his second term, Hayes helped **Republican** Ulysses S. Grant with his presidential campaign.

In 1872, Hayes left **politics**. He moved with his family to Fremont, Ohio. But soon, the Republicans wanted Hayes to be governor again. In 1875, he was elected for a third term!

Hayes helped establish the Agricultural and Mechanical College in Columbus, Ohio. It later became known as Ohio State University.

Election of 1876

In 1876, the **Republican** Party chose Hayes to run for president. He ran against **Democrat** Samuel Tilden. It was a very close race. Tilden received 184 **electoral votes**. Hayes received 165. The winner needed 185 electoral votes.

However, Democrats and Republicans in three states were arguing over who won. So, 20 electoral votes were still undecided. The matter was settled by an Electoral **Commission**. It gave the 20 electoral votes to Hayes. So, Hayes then had 185 votes and won the election!

Hayes was the only president whose election was decided by an Electoral Commission.

President Hayes

Hayes was **inaugurated** in March 1877. One of his first acts was withdrawing the US Army from Louisiana, South Carolina, and Florida. This marked the end of **Reconstruction**.

Next, Hayes wanted to improve **civil service**. He did not believe in giving government jobs to people because they helped win an election. This is called the spoils system. Hayes thought people who would do the best job should be hired.

Hayes had two inaugurations. There was a private one on March 3. His public inauguration took place on March 5.

Money was another important topic during Hayes's term. In 1878, Congress created a new act. The act would require the US government to buy silver to make silver dollars.

Hayes thought dollars should only be made of gold. So, he **vetoed** the act. However, Congress passed the act over his veto.

In addition, many people had paper money left over from the **American Civil War**. Hayes signed an act that allowed people to trade their paper dollars for gold dollars.

★ SUPREME COURT ★
APPOINTMENTS

John Marshall Harlan: 1877

William B. Woods: 1881

PRESIDENT HAYES'S CABINET

March 3, 1877–March 4, 1881

★ **STATE:** William M. Evarts
★ **TREASURY:** John Sherman
★ **WAR:** George W. McCrary, Alexander Ramsey (from December 12, 1879)
★ **NAVY:** Richard W. Thompson, Nathan Goff Jr. (from January 6, 1881)
★ **ATTORNEY GENERAL:** Charles Devens
★ **INTERIOR:** Carl Schurz

Hayes with his cabinet

Return to Ohio

Hayes did not run for a second term. His presidency ended in March 1881. Hayes and his family moved back to Ohio.

There, Hayes continued to work hard. He helped several colleges and other educational groups. Education was not the only cause Hayes worked for. He also worked to improve the prison system.

★ DID YOU KNOW? ★

Spiegel Grove is the site of the nation's first presidential library.

The Hayes home in Fremont, Ohio, is called Spiegel Grove.

Lucy Hayes died in 1889. Hayes missed his wife deeply. But he kept busy working and visiting family. Hayes became ill in January 1893. On January 17, 1893, Rutherford B. Hayes died at Spiegel Grove.

Rutherford B. Hayes was an important American leader. He worked to secure rights for African Americans. He was also in favor of improving public education and the **civil service**. Many of President Hayes's ideas paved the way for future presidents.

★ DID YOU KNOW? ★

Lucy Hayes was the first president's wife to have completed college.

Mr. and Mrs. Hayes are buried together at Spiegel Grove.

Office of the President

Branches of Government

The US government has three branches. They are the executive, legislative, and judicial branches. Each branch has some power over the others. This is called a system of checks and balances.

★ Executive Branch

The executive branch enforces laws. It is made up of the president, the vice president, and the president's cabinet. The president represents the United States around the world. He or she also signs bills into law and leads the military.

★ Legislative Branch

The legislative branch makes laws, maintains the military, and regulates trade. It also has the power to declare war. This branch includes the Senate and the House of Representatives. Together, these two houses form Congress.

★ Judicial Branch

The judicial branch interprets laws. It is made up of district courts, courts of appeals, and the Supreme Court. District courts try cases. Sometimes people disagree with a trial's outcome. Then he or she may appeal. If a court of appeals supports the ruling, a person may appeal to the Supreme Court.

Qualifications for Office

To be president, a candidate must be at least 35 years old. The person must be a natural-born US citizen. He or she must also have lived in the United States for at least 14 years.

Electoral College

The US presidential election is an indirect election. Voters from each state choose electors. These electors represent their state in the Electoral College. Each elector has one electoral vote. Electors cast their vote for the candidate with the highest number of votes from people in their state. A candidate must receive the majority of Electoral College votes to win.

Term of Office

Each president may be elected to two four-year terms. The presidential election is held on the Tuesday after the first Monday in November. The president is sworn in on January 20 of the following year. At that time, he or she takes the oath of office.
It states:

> I do solemnly swear (or affirm) that I will faithfully execute the office of President of the United States, and will to the best of my ability, preserve, protect and defend the Constitution of the United States.

31

Line of Succession

The Presidential Succession Act of 1947 states who becomes president if the president cannot serve. The vice president is first in the line. Next are the Speaker of the House and the President Pro Tempore of the Senate. It may happen that none of these individuals is able to serve. Then the office falls to the president's cabinet members. They would take office in the order in which each department was created:

Secretary of State

Secretary of the Treasury

Secretary of Defense

Attorney General

Secretary of the Interior

Secretary of Agriculture

Secretary of Commerce

Secretary of Labor

Secretary of Health and Human Services

Secretary of Housing and Urban Development

Secretary of Transportation

Secretary of Energy

Secretary of Education

Secretary of Veterans Affairs

Secretary of Homeland Security

Benefits

★ While in office, the president receives a salary. It is $400,000 per year. He or she lives in the White House. The president also has 24-hour Secret Service protection.

★ The president may travel on a Boeing 747 jet. This special jet is called Air Force One. It can hold 70 passengers. It has kitchens, a dining room, sleeping areas, and more. Air Force One can fly halfway around the world before needing to refuel. It can even refuel in flight!

★ When the president travels by car, he or she uses Cadillac One. It is a Cadillac Deville that has been modified. The car has heavy armor and communications systems. The president may even take Cadillac One along when visiting other countries.

★ The president also travels on a helicopter. It is called Marine One. It may also be taken along when the president visits other countries.

★ Sometimes the president needs to get away with family and friends. Camp David is the official presidential retreat. It is located in Maryland. The US Navy maintains the retreat. The US Marine Corps keeps it secure. The camp offers swimming, tennis, golf, and hiking.

★ When the president leaves office, he or she receives lifetime Secret Service protection. He or she also receives a yearly pension of $203,700. The former president also receives money for office space, supplies, and staff.

33

PRESIDENTS AND THEIR TERMS

PRESIDENT	PARTY	TOOK OFFICE	LEFT OFFICE	TERMS SERVED	VICE PRESIDENT
George Washington	None	April 30, 1789	March 4, 1797	Two	John Adams
John Adams	Federalist	March 4, 1797	March 4, 1801	One	Thomas Jefferson
Thomas Jefferson	Democratic-Republican	March 4, 1801	March 4, 1809	Two	Aaron Burr, George Clinton
James Madison	Democratic-Republican	March 4, 1809	March 4, 1817	Two	George Clinton, Elbridge Gerry
James Monroe	Democratic-Republican	March 4, 1817	March 4, 1825	Two	Daniel D. Tompkins
John Quincy Adams	Democratic-Republican	March 4, 1825	March 4, 1829	One	John C. Calhoun
Andrew Jackson	Democrat	March 4, 1829	March 4, 1837	Two	John C. Calhoun, Martin Van Buren
Martin Van Buren	Democrat	March 4, 1837	March 4, 1841	One	Richard M. Johnson
William H. Harrison	Whig	March 4, 1841	April 4, 1841	Died During First Term	John Tyler
John Tyler	Whig	April 6, 1841	March 4, 1845	Completed Harrison's Term	Office Vacant
James K. Polk	Democrat	March 4, 1845	March 4, 1849	One	George M. Dallas
Zachary Taylor	Whig	March 5, 1849	July 9, 1850	Died During First Term	Millard Fillmore

PRESIDENT	PARTY	TOOK OFFICE	LEFT OFFICE	TERMS SERVED	VICE PRESIDENT
Millard Fillmore	Whig	July 10, 1850	March 4, 1853	Completed Taylor's Term	Office Vacant
Franklin Pierce	Democrat	March 4, 1853	March 4, 1857	One	William R.D. King
James Buchanan	Democrat	March 4, 1857	March 4, 1861	One	John C. Breckinridge
Abraham Lincoln	Republican	March 4, 1861	April 15, 1865	Served One Term, Died During Second Term	Hannibal Hamlin, Andrew Johnson
Andrew Johnson	Democrat	April 15, 1865	March 4, 1869	Completed Lincoln's Second Term	Office Vacant
Ulysses S. Grant	Republican	March 4, 1869	March 4, 1877	Two	Schuyler Colfax, Henry Wilson
Rutherford B. Hayes	Republican	March 3, 1877	March 4, 1881	One	William A. Wheeler
James A. Garfield	Republican	March 4, 1881	September 19, 1881	Died During First Term	Chester Arthur
Chester Arthur	Republican	September 20, 1881	March 4, 1885	Completed Garfield's Term	Office Vacant
Grover Cleveland	Democrat	March 4, 1885	March 4, 1889	One	Thomas A. Hendricks
Benjamin Harrison	Republican	March 4, 1889	March 4, 1893	One	Levi P. Morton
Grover Cleveland	Democrat	March 4, 1893	March 4, 1897	One	Adlai E. Stevenson
William McKinley	Republican	March 4, 1897	September 14, 1901	Served One Term, Died During Second Term	Garret A. Hobart, Theodore Roosevelt

PRESIDENT	PARTY	TOOK OFFICE	LEFT OFFICE	TERMS SERVED	VICE PRESIDENT
Theodore Roosevelt	Republican	September 14, 1901	March 4, 1909	Completed McKinley's Second Term, Served One Term	Office Vacant, Charles Fairbanks
William Taft	Republican	March 4, 1909	March 4, 1913	One	James S. Sherman
Woodrow Wilson	Democrat	March 4, 1913	March 4, 1921	Two	Thomas R. Marshall
Warren G. Harding	Republican	March 4, 1921	August 2, 1923	Died During First Term	Calvin Coolidge
Calvin Coolidge	Republican	August 3, 1923	March 4, 1929	Completed Harding's Term, Served One Term	Office Vacant, Charles Dawes
Herbert Hoover	Republican	March 4, 1929	March 4, 1933	One	Charles Curtis
Franklin D. Roosevelt	Democrat	March 4, 1933	April 12, 1945	Served Three Terms, Died During Fourth Term	John Nance Garner, Henry A. Wallace, Harry S. Truman
Harry S. Truman	Democrat	April 12, 1945	January 20, 1953	Completed Roosevelt's Fourth Term, Served One Term	Office Vacant, Alben Barkley
Dwight D. Eisenhower	Republican	January 20, 1953	January 20, 1961	Two	Richard Nixon
John F. Kennedy	Democrat	January 20, 1961	November 22, 1963	Died During First Term	Lyndon B. Johnson
Lyndon B. Johnson	Democrat	November 22, 1963	January 20, 1969	Completed Kennedy's Term, Served One Term	Office Vacant, Hubert H. Humphrey
Richard Nixon	Republican	January 20, 1969	August 9, 1974	Completed First Term, Resigned During Second Term	Spiro T. Agnew, Gerald Ford

PRESIDENT	PARTY	TOOK OFFICE	LEFT OFFICE	TERMS SERVED	VICE PRESIDENT
Gerald Ford	Republican	August 9, 1974	January 20, 1977	Completed Nixon's Second Term	Nelson A. Rockefeller
Jimmy Carter	Democrat	January 20, 1977	January 20, 1981	One	Walter Mondale
Ronald Reagan	Republican	January 20, 1981	January 20, 1989	Two	George H.W. Bush
George H.W. Bush	Republican	January 20, 1989	January 20, 1993	One	Dan Quayle
Bill Clinton	Democrat	January 20, 1993	January 20, 2001	Two	Al Gore
George W. Bush	Republican	January 20, 2001	January 20, 2009	Two	Dick Cheney
Barack Obama	Democrat	January 20, 2009	January 20, 2017	Two	Joe Biden

"He serves his party best who serves his country best." Rutherford B. Hayes

★ WRITE TO THE PRESIDENT ★

You may write to the president at:
The White House
1600 Pennsylvania Avenue NW
Washington, DC 20500

You may e-mail the president at:
comments@whitehouse.gov

37

Glossary

amendment—a change to a country's or a state's constitution.

American Civil War—the war between the Northern and Southern states from 1861 to 1865.

civil service—the part of the government that is responsible for matters not covered by the military, the courts, or the law.

commission—a group of people who meet to solve a particular problem or do certain tasks.

constitution (kahnt-stuh-TOO-shuhn)—the basic laws that govern a country or a state.

Democrat—a member of the Democratic political party.

electoral vote—a vote cast by a member of the Electoral College for the candidate who received the most popular votes in his or her state.

impeach—to charge someone for doing wrong while serving in a public office.

inaugurate—to swear into a political office.

politics—the art or science of government. Something referring to politics is political. A person who is active in politics is a politician.

Reconstruction—the period after the American Civil War when laws were passed to help the Southern states rebuild and return to the Union.

representative—someone chosen in an election to act or speak for the people who voted for him or her.

Republican—a member of the Republican political party.

Secretary of War—a member of the president's cabinet who handled the military and national defense.

solicitor—the chief law officer of a city, town, county, or government division.

Union—the Northern states that remained part of the United States during the American Civil War.

university—a school a student may attend after finishing high school. A university is often made up of several colleges.

veto—the right of one member of a decision-making group to stop an action by the group.

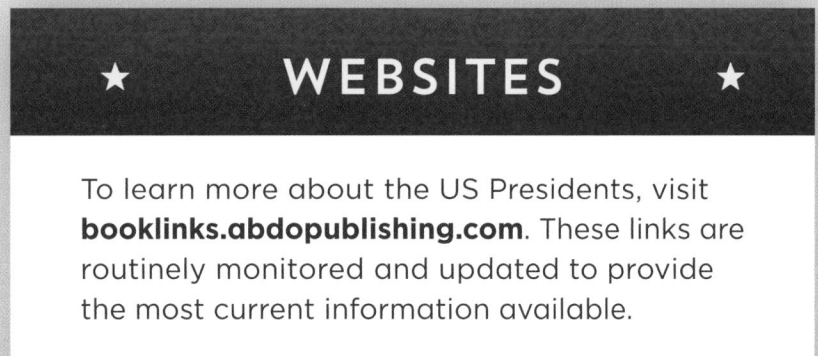

WEBSITES

★ ★

To learn more about the US Presidents, visit **booklinks.abdopublishing.com**. These links are routinely monitored and updated to provide the most current information available.

Index